A Door That's Never Locked

A children's guide to visiting the Ohel

Malka Touger

אהל מרנא ורבנא
כ"ק אדמו"ר הרה"ק נ"ע שניאורסאהן
יוסף יצחק נ"ע מליובאוויטש

מנחם מענדל
אהל

A Door that's Never Locked
A Children's Guide to Visiting the Ohel

Editor: Suri Brand
Photographs: Shuki Greenberg
Cover: D. Liff
Graphic Assistance: Rivki Werdiger
Cover Photo: Levi Liberow
Pictures of the Rebbe: The Avner Institute

Published by
Merkos L'Inyonei Chinuch
770 Eastern Parkway / Brooklyn, New York 11213
(718) 774-4000 / FAX (718) 774-2718
editor@kehot.com

Order Department:
291 Kingston Avenue / Brooklyn, New York 11213
(718) 778-0226 / FAX (718) 778-4148
www.kehot.com

ISBN: 978-0-8266-0131-5

Printed in Israel

CONTENTS

Publisher's Foreword

We are pleased to present *A Door that's Never Locked: A Children's Guide to Visiting the Ohel*.

As more and more people, including children, are introduced to the significance of visiting the Ohel - the resting place of the Lubavitcher Rebbe, Rabbi Menachem M. Schneerson, and that of his predecessor, Rabbi Yosef Yitzchak of Lubavitch, of blessed memory - it has become apparent that there is a pressing need for a book that will help children gain a deeper understanding of these visits.

Noted educator Mrs. Malka Touger has accomplished the intricate task of presenting this material in an easy-to-read narrative, managing to keep the delicate balance of conveying profound concepts while keeping it simple enough to engage the youthful reader. Indeed, many adults will find new insights and a keener understanding of the soulful encounter that is a visit to the Ohel.*

In consultation with an array of Rabbinical and educational authorities, the book is rounded out by the addition of *My First Maaneh Lashon*, suggested prayers culled from *Maaneh Lashon*, published by the Kehot Publication Society.

Merkos L'Inyonei Chinuch

---

* An in-depth exploration is available in *Staying the Course*, Chasidic Heritage Series (Kehot, 2011).

Author's Introduction

The sweet-faced little boy pointing diligently to each word of the *Tehillim* caught my attention as I entered the Ohel. *If only all children could sense the value of these precious moments,* I thought to myself.

And why not? What would it take to arouse their interest and connection to this place, so dear to our hearts?

Not much, I concluded. *Children have a natural sensitivity to kedushah. All we have to do is provide guidance and direction.*

Guidance! That's it! What if there were a guide for a child's visit to the Ohel? Something that would help him or her prepare, as well as provide a text for children to read from at the tziyun.

From those random thoughts, this book was born. Its purpose is to prepare and thus enrich a child's visit to the Ohel and to suggest a "first" *Maaneh Lashon* that he or she can recite. This may ease his or her path to ultimately being able to say the entire *Maaneh Lashon* as established by the Mittler Rebbe, Rabbi Dov Ber of Lubavitch, to be recited at the *tziyun* of his father, the Alter Rebbe, Rabbi Schneur Zalman of Liadi.

Though it is written as a children's book, children may not pick up this book on their own. Before the visit to the Ohel, you can set aside some quiet and contemplative time to read the book to a child or together with him or her. The book does not have to be read in one sitting. It is divided by subtitles and lends itself to being read in parts. This is even advisable, because there is much information that the child may need time to absorb due to the nature and sensitivity of the topic. You may also want to take time to talk with your child and share your own feelings.

Much research has been done in the process of clarifying many issues explained in the book. Many people have contributed to this process, and their knowledge and enthusiasm for the project served as a prod, continually pushing it forward.

Among the many consulted were:

Rabbi Moshe Bogomilsky, Rabbi Alter Eliyahu Friedman, Rabbi Yosef B. Friedman, Rabbi Menachem Mendel Gluckowsky, Rabbi Leibel Groner, Rabbi Menachem Mendel Groner, Rabbi Binyamin Klein, Rabbi Yehuda Krinsky, Rabbi Levi Yitzchak Raskin, Rabbi Abba Refson, Rabbi Eliyahu Touger, and Rabbi Sholom Ber Wineberg.

Among the many who offered *chinuch* and editorial insights:

Rabbi Sholom Baras, Rabbi Menachem Mendel Greenbaum, Mrs. Menucha Kaplan, Uri Kaploun, Mrs. Bluma Marcus, Mrs. Natalia Thalheim, Naomi Touger and Mrs. Sarah Michal Touger.

Photographs of children at the Ohel were included to help bring the Ohel experience closer to a child's heart. Many thanks to all whose pictures feature in the book:

Mendel Azimov; Rabbi Mendy and Levi Baras; Shaina Brook; Mendel Duchman; Rabbi Moshe Feller; Chaya, Bina, and Hadassah Greenberg; Menny Greenberg; Dr. Chaim Gross; Rabbi Chaim, Shmuly, and Nachum Gurevitch; Mussie Lehrer; Mendel Shemtov; Mendel, Zalmy, and Levi Touger; and Shterna and Tamara Vogel.

Many thanks to the Shemtov Family for appreciating the need for this book and enabling it to become a reality. This book is dedicated to the memory of their esteemed parents, Reb Menachem Mendel ben Reb Benzion Shemtov and Mrs. Sarah bas Reb Yakov Efraim HaCohen Shemtov.

It is my sincere hope that this book will become immediately unnecessary, because we will have merited the geulah with the coming of Moshiach now!

Malka Touger

Yerushalayim

Yud Alef Nissan 5771

A
GUIDE TO
VISITING
THE
OHEL

A Most Special Opportunity

RRRRING!

"It's probably another reservation," Yossi thought as his mother reached for the phone.

He was right. One more person wanted to sign up for tomorrow's trip. "We may need another bus," Mrs. Cohen murmured as she hung up the receiver.

For a Tuesday night, the phone in the Cohen home had been ringing more than usual – and "usual" in the busy shluchim's household meant a lot of calls! But tonight, to eight-year-old Yossi, it seemed like it had been ringing nonstop.

"Mommy," he said, "lots of people are coming with us to the Ohel. I know that it's something our family does, but I didn't think that so many other people would want to go, too."

His mother looked at him with a sober expression. "Yossi, you sound as if you think that the Ohel is a place that only some people want to visit. But many people know how special the Ohel is and want to have the chance to go. In fact, visiting the resting place of tzaddikim is not a new kind of Chabad House activity. It's something that Jews have done for thousands of years. Do you remember the *dvar Torah* that Mendy said at the Shabbos table last week?"

Mendy was Yossi's older brother. "Yes, Mommy," said Yossi, "I remember. He spoke about the *meraglim* – the spies that Moshe sent to Eretz Yisrael."

"That's right. And he talked about one of the first people who knew how helpful it can be to daven at the resting place of tzaddikim."

"I know who that was!" Yossi said excitedly. "It was Calev!"

"Yes, he made a detour to Chevron so that he could visit *Me'aras HaMachpelah*, where our *Avos* are buried. There he davened that he should be protected from the bad influence of the other spies.[1] And he wasn't the only example. The Talmud mentions many great sages who visited the resting places of tzaddikim. There are also many stories of Jews who prayed at such places and asked HaShem that their tefillos be accepted because holy people are buried there."

Yossi's forehead wrinkled in puzzlement. "What do you mean?"

"Do you remember when Auntie Esther and Uncle Yanky traveled to Israel last year?"

Yossi nodded. "They went to visit our cousins, but they also wanted to daven for Zaidy, who was very sick. They went to pray for him at the Kosel and at places where tzaddikim are buried."

"That special holiness helps a person's davening."

"They traveled all that way there because of the holiness of those places. That special holiness helps a person's davening. It's like davening to HaShem when you are standing right in front of Him."

"But doesn't HaShem hear all of our tefillos no matter where we are?"

"Yes, but davening in a holy place is different. Remember when you told me that you went to speak to the principal because of the problem you were having on the bus ride to school?"

Yossi frowned at the memory. "A bigger kid wouldn't let me sit where I wanted and kept pushing me off the seat. The safety guard said it would be best to tell the principal. I had to ask my teacher to go to the secretary to ask the principal when I could speak to him in his office."

"That's a lot of people to talk to just to get an appointment!"

Yossi grinned. "Remember what happened in the end? At recess, I saw the principal standing in the doorway of his office. I must have been staring at him because he motioned me to come inside, and I was able to talk to him without making the appointment. That kid never bothered me again."

"I'm glad of that!" said Mrs. Cohen. "What happened with the principal is a good way to understand why davening at a holy place makes our prayers more powerful. When we daven to HaShem, we have to be truthful and really mean what we say. It has to come from deep inside of us. Often we have to work hard to reach that deep place.

"But there are times when our minds wander and our davening is not so sincere. Those tefillos also go up to HaShem, but the angels must help them along – just like you had to ask one person after another before you could speak to the principal. But when we are in a holy place, the holiness helps the deep part inside of us come out. We connect to HaShem more directly.[2] The resting place of a tzaddik is also holy. That's why people will travel very far to daven at the resting place of a tzaddik."

"I knew the Ohel was a special place, but I didn't realize how special," admitted Yossi. "No wonder so many people want to go."

"Visiting cemeteries has always been a part of Jewish life. We are comfortable with the idea, and we even call it a *beis hachayim*, a place for the living," added his mother.

"Azkir al HaTziyun –

I Will Mention This at the Tziyun"

© The Avner Institute

As Yossi thought about cemeteries being called a "place for the living," his mother interrupted his thoughts with a question.

"Yossi, can you think of a great person in recent times who often went to the Ohel?"

"Of course! I have pictures of the Rebbe at the Ohel in my collection."

"Yes. The Rebbe visited the Ohel, because it is the resting place of his father-in-law, the Frierdike Rebbe. The Rebbe considered davening at the Ohel so special that when people would ask for a blessing, many times the answer would be '*Azkir al hatziyun* – I will mention this [for a blessing] at the *tziyun*.' He took many of the letters and requests for blessings with him and read them at the *tziyun*. And we know that he once wrote in a letter to a chassid, 'I am surprised that you overlooked the opportunity to go to the Ohel.'[3] The previous Rebbes did the same."[4]

"I guess it does make sense that people would want to go to the Ohel, in that case. But why did the Rebbe call it the '*tziyun*'? You told me it's the 'Ohel,' and isn't that what everyone else calls it, too?"

Mrs. Cohen smiled. "You have sharp ears, Yossi! The truth is, we use both names, *tziyun* and Ohel. *Tziyun* is the Hebrew word for 'marker' – something that marks the resting place.

"An *ohel* is a structure. From the earliest times, it has been a custom to build a structure over the burial place of a tzaddik.[5] It is called an '*ohel*' because that is the halachic term for a covering over a place where a person is buried. Interestingly, the word *ohel* shares the same root letters as the phrase '*behilo neiro*,' which means 'his light shines forth.'[6] This is a place where a tzaddik's light shines forth."[7]

As his mother spoke about the meaning of the word *ohel*, Yossi suddenly remembered something. "But my teacher in school taught us that an *ohel* is a tent. We learned that when he told us about Avraham Avinu's tent, which had four doors so that he could welcome guests."

"Yes, Yossi, an *ohel* also means a 'tent.' People stay in a tent for short periods of time."

"Like the tent we used in the summer for the camp Shabbaton. I never thought so many kids could fit in one tent! It was so much fun!"

"We had a great turnout, didn't we!" his mother agreed, smiling. "The tent was fine for the weekend, but it's not a place you'd want to live in all the time. We are taught that the word *ohel* hints at the body and all its physical needs and wants.[8] As we know, a body is not permanent. It is a temporary house – like a tent – for the neshamah. A resting place in the *beis hachayim* is also like a tent because it is not permanent. In the very near future, Moshiach will come, and the neshamos will leave their resting places and come back. The word *ohel* helps us remember that this resting place is temporary."

Even More…

Mrs. Cohen paused and glanced at Yossi. He had suddenly become very quiet, and he was biting his lip, as if he was trying to put together the pieces of a puzzle.

"Do you understand now, Yossi, why going to the Ohel is so important to many people, and not just our family?"

"Yes, Mommy, I understand, but –"

"What is it?"

"Today I asked my friend Danny if he wanted to sit with me on the bus tomorrow. He told me that he's not going on the trip."

Yossi's mother pulled up a chair and beckoned him to sit next to her.

"I can understand why Danny doesn't want to go," she said softly. "Even though many adults visit the resting places of holy people or their parents and grandparents, they don't always take children along. Yet when it came to seeing the Rebbe, people always took their children."

"But that was before Gimmel Tamuz!" Yossi protested.

"Yossi, people came to the Rebbe to be in the presence of a holy tzaddik. That doesn't change. Being near the Rebbe brings us closer to HaShem[9] and gives our neshamos more strength.[10] From the *Zohar,* we can understand that the Rebbe can affect us now even more powerfully than before.[11] That's why we go to the Ohel. When Danny learns more about this, he may understand it better."

"But how can that be?" Yossi asked. "How can the Rebbe affect us more now?"

Just then, Yossi's little sister Chani burst into the kitchen like a whirlwind.

"Mommy," she wailed, "I'm so thirsty I could drink up the whole ocean!"

"We can't have that! I'll get you a drink of water," Mrs. Cohen offered.

"But I'm really only thirsty for orange juice," Chani insisted.

Yossi hid a smile as his mother poured a cup of juice and handed it to Chani. The little girl recited the berachah, gulped down the juice, made an after-berachah, and ran out again.

Making the Right Connections

Mrs. Cohen turned back to Yossi. "Did you notice how much juice I poured into Chani's cup?" she asked. "I wouldn't have minded giving her more juice. She was very thirsty, it's healthy, and we have plenty. But I only gave her a certain amount."

Yossi looked at his mother quizzically. "Well, you didn't want her to spill it, right?"

"Yes, that's true, but even if I poured the juice up to the brim, I couldn't fill the cup with more juice than it can hold."

"Of course not. It would spill all over the table."

"It certainly would. If you think about it, the juice and the cup can teach us about the neshamah and the body."

Yossi blinked his eyes. "Huh?"

"The neshamah is still a part of HaShem, so it is endless and unlimited, just like HaShem."

"HaShem has unlimited power, like we have lots of orange juice. HaShem gives of His power to our neshamos. Then He 'pours' the neshamah's power into our body just like we pour the juice into the cup. This allows our body to think, feel, speak, and act the way our neshamah wants it to. But even though it is in the body, the neshamah is still a part of HaShem, so it is endless and unlimited, just like HaShem.

"And just as the cup cannot hold all of the juice that is in the bottle, the body cannot feel and express everything the whole neshamah can express. We can think deeply and understand a lot, but we can't understand everything our neshamah knows. We can feel strongly and speak very clearly, but we cannot express everything our neshamah would like to say. And we cannot go everywhere and do everything our neshamah would like to do. Our body limits the power of the neshamah to express itself, like the cup that limits the amount of juice it can hold."

The picture of a tall glass overflowing with orange juice jumped into Yossi's mind. Then he thought about a body holding a neshamah that is too powerful for it to contain. "Wow, Mommy! I never thought of it like that."

"Now, a tzaddik is on a high level, and his body does not

limit his neshamah in the same way that other people are limited. He can see more than regular people can see with their eyes and understand and feel much more, too. Yet even when the neshamah of a tzaddik is in his body, there are some limitations, and sometimes it's hard for *us* to connect to his holiness."

"What do you mean?" asked Yossi.

"One example of this on a very simple level is that when a person wanted to go into *yechidus*, a private time with the Rebbe, he had to make an appointment. And the line for dollars that you see on the videos took hours. Not everyone could see the Rebbe at the same time."

"Oh, I get it!" exclaimed Yossi. "Now many people can connect to the Rebbe at the same time."

"That's right. What's more, the *Zohar* teaches us that we can connect to the Rebbe on a higher level now, after Gimmel Tamuz, than we could in the past. When his neshamah was in his body, we could connect to the Rebbe only up to a certain point. But now his neshamah soars very high and can shine that holiness upon us when we make the effort to connect.

"The *Zohar* teaches us that during this temporary and short time before the *geulah*, we can connect with the Rebbe's holiness because it shines without the limitations of a body. This is why going to the Ohel and working on *hiskashrus*, making that connection, is so important. The Rebbe once told a chassid that strong feelings of connection help a chassid be open and receive blessings and help in the areas he needs it."[12]

"Mommy, all this sounds interesting, and I understand it much better now. What should I do so that I'll think and feel all the things we are talking about, when we are at the Ohel?"

Mrs. Cohen reached out to squeeze her son's hand. "That's a mature attitude, Yossi! I am really proud that you want to make your visit to the Ohel more meaningful. Tomorrow you will have a chance to make that happen. When you are standing at the Ohel, picture yourself standing before the Rebbe. Concentrate on connecting to the powerful light of HaShem and, in this holy place, ask that your tefillos should be answered. Our tefillos at the Ohel are very powerful. As the Rebbe himself said, 'It is effective. Even if we don't understand how it works, it does.' "[13]

A Tzaddik's Holiness Is Always Shining

The next day was bright and sunny, a good day for a long trip. Yossi had gotten the best seat on the bus – close to the front so that he had a view of the huge windshield. He missed Danny, but he was happy to see that another friend, Josh, had joined his parents on the trip.

"Hi, Yossi!" Josh called. "Do you want to sit together?"

Yossi nodded and moved over, glad to have someone to talk to on the long bus ride. And Josh had lots to say. He had just returned from a family trip to Eretz Yisrael and was bubbling with excitement about his experiences.

"I've never been to the Ohel," Josh said. "Before I went to Israel, I didn't think I would want to go. But we went to so many places where holy people are buried I got used to it, and it doesn't feel strange anymore. It was actually fun. We did a lot of climbing on the way – some of the places we went to were on mountaintops, and some were down in valleys. And there was this one place in an unfriendly Arab area. An army jeep had to drive behind our bus to protect us."

"Sounds neat," Yossi commented. "Well, at least here in America, the Ohel is easy to get to."

"You can say that again! But you know, after praying at all those places in Israel, I wonder why the Ohel is not there, too. The Ohel of a holy person should be in the Holy Land, don't you think? Our guide in Israel told us that some people who didn't even live in Israel are buried there."

"I'm not sure why the Ohel isn't in Israel," said Yossi. "But I know of another great Jewish leader who is not buried in Israel either."

"Who?"

"Moshe Rabbeinu. He was buried in the desert, the place where he was the people's leader."[14]

Josh grinned. "Oh, right, I knew that. And wasn't there another leader who wasn't buried in the Holy Land at first and then he was brought later? I think I learned about it in Hebrew school."

Yossi nodded. "That was Yosef. His body was buried in Egypt for many years so that he could be near the Jewish people while they were in Egypt. My teacher told us that because the people knew that his resting place was close it helped them get through the really hard times."

"I think I can explain something about the neshamah of a tzaddik and the holiness of Eretz Yisrael."

"I don't mean to eavesdrop, boys, but I overheard your conversation and I think I can explain something about the neshamah of a tzaddik and the holiness of Eretz Yisrael."

The offer came from across the aisle, from Shmuly, a yeshivah student who helped out at the Chabad House. Yossi and Josh turned to him expectantly.

"We know that Eretz Yisrael has a special holiness that no

other land has," Shmuly said. "But until Moshiach comes, the holiness in Eretz Yisrael doesn't shine as brightly as it did in the times of the Beis HaMikdash. Still, the destruction of the Temple affected only the holiness that people could see and feel. There is always holiness in the land that is not affected by anything, and we can sense it when we connect with it there.

"It's the same, and even more so, with the neshamah of a tzaddik. There are some tzaddikim who are on a very high level and are not affected by the destruction of the Beis HaMikdash. When you daven at their graves, it is like davening in Eretz Yisrael when the Beis HaMikdash still stood."[15]

A Special Kind of Davening

Now Yossi had a question.

"I've been wondering about that. My teacher taught us that the Tzemach Tzedek said, '*Mach dah Eretz Yisrael*'[16] – that we should make the holiness of Eretz Yisrael shine wherever we are in the world. He explained that Eretz Yisrael is not just a place on the map. It's a place where HaShem's holiness rests. By doing mitzvos, we bring HaShem's holiness into the world, and this makes every place holy. If the holiness of the Rebbe's neshamah is compared to the holiness of Eretz Yisrael, why do people even have to go to the Ohel? Our Chabad House people have to drive for hours to get there, and a lot of people come from even further away. Why don't we just try to connect to the holiness from wherever we are?"

"That's a good question, Yossi," agreed Josh. "I never thought about it, but now that you asked, I would like to know the answer, too."

Shmuly was pleased. "Boys, I'm impressed with your thoughtful and serious attitude toward going to the Ohel. It's good to be thinking about where we are going and why. Let me share some ideas with you that may answer your question.

"We know that a part of a person's neshamah remains at the place where he is buried and doesn't depart from there.[17] So the Ohel is the best place to daven and make a connection with the special holiness of the tzaddik. The power of our davening at the Ohel is not the same as when we daven somewhere else.

"As we stand at the *tziyun*, we think about the greatness of the Rebbe and the holy part of the neshamah that still hovers there. This reminds us how small we are, and we feel more humble.[18] This feeling helps us daven with more *kavanah* and earnestness. Do you understand what I mean?"

Yossi nodded.

"That makes sense," said Josh.

"And here's something else to think about: chassidim feel a strong longing for the Rebbe at the Ohel. This longing causes us to daven with more feeling, which makes our tefillos more effective.[19] And, as we said before, our tefillos are also more effective at the Ohel because there we connect to the power of the Rebbe's neshamah. Since his neshamah is no longer limited to the body, it takes our tefillos to a higher place. So when we are at the Ohel, our tefillos can actually reach further."[20]

"Hmm, thanks Shmuly," said Yossi. "You gave me a lot to think about when I daven at the Ohel."

Shmuly smiled. "I have a feeling that this time you might daven differently than before. What do you think?"

The look on Yossi's face showed he understood.

"This is exactly what the Rebbe taught us. Since we know that the power of tefillah at this place is very great, our tefillos at the Ohel can be more sincere and heartfelt."[21]

Making the Most of Our Visit

Josh opened his mouth to say something, but whatever he might have said had to wait. Yossi's father stood up and spoke through the bus's loudspeaker.

"My friends," said Rabbi Cohen, "I hope that you are having a pleasant ride, and I apologize if I am interrupting your conversations."

Everyone on the bus stopped talking and turned to look at Rabbi Cohen. Yossi sat up and peeked at his father over the high seat in front of him.

"A few people sitting near me have been asking some questions, and people sitting a few rows behind requested to join the conversation. I assume that others may be interested in the things we have been talking about. Even though we learned about the merit and value of going to the Ohel in our class last week, I would like to take a few minutes to share some more ideas with you."

With a feeling of pride, Yossi settled back in his seat to hear what his father had to say.

"We are very grateful to have an opportunity to visit the Ohel. You see, beyond our efforts to connect to a tzaddik and daven, just visiting places where holy people are buried is very helpful and important. For example, the Torah says that a *kohen* is not allowed to be near a grave. But the Rabbis instructed us how to build the Ohel in a way that a *kohen* can reach it and will not miss the benefit of visiting this holy place.[22] You will notice the mesh gate that lines the walkway to the Ohel. This provides the required separation, allowing a *kohen* to walk through. Inside the Ohel, a low stone wall around the *tziyun* serves the same purpose. *Kohanim* should take care not to extend their hands over the wall.

"We are taught that the *tziyun* of a tzaddik is connected to the Cave of Machpelah in Chevron, where our *Avos* are buried. This connects us to the holiness of Eretz Yisrael.[23] And not only do we benefit personally from our visit, but we can also draw blessing for our entire family with our prayers.[24]

"Someone asked me why I am wearing my *kapote* and *gartel* – the long coat and sash you usually see me wearing on Shabbos and holidays. Important events call for preparation. Some people prepare for this visit by dressing in their special clothes. But what we wear is not what's most important. What is most important is to prepare ourselves by focusing on what we will say and do, so that we can make the most of this visit.

"And to conclude," Yossi's father added with a smile, "the Rebbe once mentioned something about the Ohel that I think about whenever I go there. He said that it brings *simchah*, joy."[25]

> "What is most important is to prepare ourselves by focusing on what we will say and do, so that we can make the most of this visit."

At the Ohel

The bus was slowing down and soon pulled to a stop. They had arrived.

After the bus had parked, Yossi's father directed the group to go ahead to the Ohel. Yossi and Josh clambered off the bus and saw Shmuly leading the way.

"Where did your father disappear to?" Josh whispered to Yossi.

Shmuly overheard Josh's question and turned around to answer him. "Rabbi Cohen went to the mikvah. Before a chassid goes to the Ohel, it is proper to go to the mikvah. When people signed up for the trip, he asked if any men wanted to go. But all this is new to many of those who came on the trip today, so I guess not everyone was ready to do that. I arranged with Rabbi Cohen that I

would lead the group until he arrives, and then I will go to the mikvah. It's nearby and he'll be back very soon. In the meantime, there are other preparations we can do."

Yossi led Josh up the stairs to the house that served as an entranceway to the Ohel.

"Where are we going?" asked Josh. "Who lives here?"

"No one – at least, not anymore," said Yossi. "It used to be a regular house, but now it is part of the whole Ohel complex. The first time I came I was also surprised. My father told me that our Rabbis taught that it is a good idea to make a place of prayer and study right next to the resting place of a tzaddik.[26] So there is a shul, a yeshivah, a children's school, and a large hall for Torah lectures, children's rallies, and events. This way people can really benefit from the holiness of the Ohel.

"They even have a Chabad House inside so people have someone they can talk to, to ask questions and learn more about Jewish things."

Walking near the boys were a father and son. Josh saw that the boy was clutching his tefillin bag tightly and kept adjusting the black hat on his head. He couldn't decide if the boy looked nervous or excited, or both.

Yossi noticed Josh staring in the boy's direction. "He's probably here to celebrate the first time he puts on tefillin in preparation for his bar mitzvah. This is something that some people do at the Ohel."

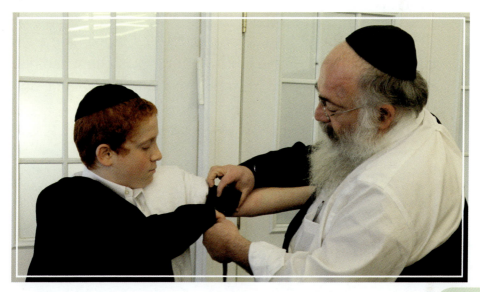

The boys joined other people in the entrance room of the house. They were watching a video of the Rebbe.

"Seeing the Rebbe and hearing him speak gets you into the right mood," Yossi said to Josh. "It reminds us why we came."

The boys walked through the small house and entered a large outdoor hall.

"Hey!" exclaimed Josh. "Look at those snacks!" He eyed the drinks and cookies on the tables. "Yum! I wish they had had this at the places we visited in Israel. After all that walking and climbing, I was so hungry."

"You'd be even more hungry if you were fasting today!" said Yossi.

"Who's fasting?"

"My father explained that many people don't eat anything on the day they go to the Ohel until after the visit.[27] Even though they do drink,[28] they're pretty hungry by the time they finish davening. That's what the food is here for, and everyone can have some."

"Actually, sometimes they do serve meals. People hold farbrengens and Shabbatons here — you know, like the ones we have at our Chabad House."

"But what are the long tables for?" asked Josh. "It's not like they're serving a big meal here or anything. It's just a few snacks."

"Actually, sometimes they do serve meals. People hold *farbrengens* and Shabbatons here – you know, like the ones we have at our Chabad House. But the tables are also here so that people can sit down and write a special note that they will read at the *tziyun*."

"What kind of note?"

"It's like a letter. You write down what you're davening for. It's called a *'pan.'* "

"Oh, like the notes people write and put into the Western Wall in Jerusalem?" asked Josh.

"Yes, but here we read the note quietly while we daven, and then tear it. That was what the Rebbe would do when he davened at the Ohel and read the letters that people sent him."

Writing the *Pan*

"What did you call it – a *'pan'*? What does that mean?"

Yossi wasn't really sure why it was called a *'pan.'* He just knew that this was what it was called. But he noticed that Shmuly happened to be talking about it to the group. "Let's see what Shmuly has to say about it. He'll explain it better than I can."

"The letter you write is a personal note," Shmuly was saying. "It's called a *'pan.'* The Hebrew word *pan* is short for *pidyon nefesh*, which means 'redemption of the soul.' We are asking HaShem that our souls be redeemed from Divine judgment.

"The word redemption here can also mean allowing us to feel free. We would all like to be able to feel free to do what HaShem wants us to do with our lives, but we have things that hold us back from doing that. We want to be healthy, have a nice family, and be able to buy what we need. We can ask for these things and write them down in our *pan*. By tearing the *pan*, and dropping the pieces on top of the *tziyun*, it remains private."

"That sounds a bit strange to me," commented Josh. "I can understand why you should read what you wrote in the letter, but why leave it there?"

"Let me try to explain it to you in the Rebbe's words," offered Shmuly. "Once, after a local convention, the shluchim of South

America sent a letter to the Rebbe. The Rebbe was pleased to receive their letter but stated that because it was a very busy time, he did not have the chance to read it right away. He assured the shluchim that sending the letter had already had an effect because it had been brought to the Ohel of his father-in-law, the Rebbe Rayatz. The Rebbe said that putting the note there was like feeding information to a computer. As soon as the computer receives information, it produces results. If that's how it works for a machine, surely – and even more so – whatever is brought to the Rebbe's *tziyun* will have an effect."[29]

Just then Yossi's father returned to the group. "My dear friends," he said, "when writing your *pan,* don't think only about past mistakes and difficulties. Think about the good things that you want in your life right now. Most important, focus on the better person you want to become.[30] Don't forget to sign it using your Hebrew name and the name of your mother."

Josh looked around, then leaned over and whispered to Yossi. "See

that man sitting at the table near the pole? It doesn't look like he is writing anything. He's just reading a book."

Yossi glanced over his shoulder. "He's not reading," he whispered back to Josh. "He is learning from a book that has the Rebbe's teachings in it. I know, because my father often does that before he writes his *pan*. It's a way of preparing for going inside the Ohel."[31]

After they had written their notes, Yossi helped Josh find a pair of slippers to change into. People either came wearing non-leather shoes, or they changed into slippers supplied at the Ohel. This is done out of respect for the holiness of the site, in the same

way Moshe Rabbeinu removed his shoes when he came close to HaShem's holiness at the burning bush.

As the group walked down the pathway, Josh noticed some people nearby standing in prayer.

"Is that it?" he asked.

"No, that's the resting place of the Rebbe's wife, Rebbetzin Chaya Mushkah. Further on, the Rebbe's mother, Rebbetzin Chana, is buried," replied Yossi. "The Rebbe always stopped there whenever he came to the Ohel."

At the Tziyun

Close to the entrance to the *tziyun*, Yossi's father pointed to a large tzedakah box.

"The most important preparation for going to the Ohel is thinking about how to better ourselves and make this world ready for Moshiach. The Rebbe taught us to always include the three ways of making this world a holy place: learning Torah, praying, and giving tzedakah. We have been learning about the meaning of this visit, and we are about to pray. Giving tzedakah shows that we are willing to think about others, share what we have, and bring more goodness into the world."

People in the group reached into their pockets and dropped coins and bills into the tzedakah boxes. Now they were ready to enter the Ohel.

"Do you smell something burning in here, or am I just imagining it?" Josh asked.

Yossi's father pointed to a stand by the wall. "You're not imagining it. There is a custom to light a candle at the *tziyun* of a tzaddik. The neshamah is called a 'lamp of HaShem.'[32] A certain level of the neshamah is always present at the *tziyun* and the Rebbe would always light a candle when he came here."

Just before they entered the place of prayer by the *tziyun*, Rabbi Cohen knocked on the door. Josh turned to Yossi in surprise.

"My father knocks on the door because he saw the Rebbe do that," Yossi whispered. "I think he does it out of respect for this holy place – he's announcing himself before entering instead of just walking right in."[33]

Josh noticed some of the adults taking booklets.

He tapped Shmuly, who was standing in front of him. "What's in that book? Should I take one?"

Shmuly took a booklet from the shelf and handed it to Josh. "This booklet contains the prayers that people say at the Ohel. It is called 'Maaneh Lashon.' The name is taken from a verse in the book of Mishlei,[34] which was written by Shlomo HaMelech. The words mean that we recognize that HaShem gave us the gift of speech, and He gives us the ability to speak to Him when we daven and say Tehillim."

"That's good, because I wasn't sure what prayers I should say here," said Josh. "Does everyone say the same thing?"

"This is the booklet that the Rebbe davened from when he came here, and this is what we say. It was compiled by Rabbi Yaakov, the son of Rabbi Avraham Shlomo Shinna, and was accepted by Jews all over. It was first published in Prague in 5370 (1610) and reprinted many, many times in Hebrew and Yiddish, with only some small changes. Our edition is the one that the second Lubavitcher Rebbe, Rabbi Dov Ber, established to be recited at the tziyun of his father, Rabbi Schneur Zalman, the founder of Chabad."

"When you get older, you will find it easier to recite the original *Maaneh Lashon.* For now, say as much as you can."

"Do I have to say all of it?" Josh asked hesitantly.

"Actually, what I gave you is a version of the *Maaneh Lashon* that has been suggested for children because it is shorter. When you get older, you will find it easier to recite the original *Maaneh Lashon.* For now, say as much as you can from this booklet and follow the instructions for reading your letter."

Clutching their booklets, the boys joined the group inside, ready and prepared for their own special Ohel experience.

A Private Place for the Public

"I liked reading from that booklet," Josh said to Yossi as they walked out. "It has a lot of the things that I wanted to say, but I wouldn't have known how to say them right. When we were in Israel, I didn't know what to pray at the graves we visited, I just stood quietly and waited for everyone else to finish. I'm glad you told me what to do."

Yossi nodded shyly.

"But why was it so quiet in there?" Josh asked. "In Israel, people usually prayed out loud. Sometimes they chanted or even cried. They did it softly, but you could still hear them."

Yossi was surprised by Josh's question. He never thought that the Ohel should be anything but a quiet place. But he didn't know why. Luckily his father was walking behind the boys and overheard the question.

"Perhaps the hushed tone at the Ohel tells us a lot about how we feel when we come here," Rabbi Cohen suggested. "A chassid who comes to the Ohel is going to his Rebbe. It is like *yechidus*, a private time when you are alone with the Rebbe. You quiet the busy thoughts in your mind, and you empty your heart of the feelings that are getting in the way of your concentration. You are now open to connect to the Rebbe and absorb the holiness of this special place."

The path leading back was very narrow. Yossi squeezed beside his father, and Josh walked in front of them.

"Tatie," Yossi said, "this trip to the Ohel was really special for me. I thought about all of the –"

"It is like yechidus, a private time when you are alone with the Rebbe."

But his father didn't seem to hear him. He looked like he was deep in thought.

"Tatie, is there something wrong?"

Rabbi Cohen stroked Yossi's head. He cleared his throat and said softly, "No, Yossi. Everything is, *baruch HaShem*, fine. You know Yossi, I am very proud of you. You may not have noticed, but I was paying attention to the way you have been helping Josh and teaching him. Mommy also told me about the good questions you asked her. It is important that we understand what a visit to the Ohel is all about, and to appreciate what a berachah and *zchus* it is to be able to daven at the Ohel. But we really want more. We want Moshiach to come, and we want to have the Rebbe with us right now."

Yossi understood. He nodded and wished it were so with all his heart. He and his father walked away from the Ohel hand in hand.

When they were back inside the building where they had written their *pan*, Yossi led Josh to the sinks so they could wash their hands. "You're supposed to wash your hands whenever you leave a cemetery," Yossi explained.

On the way back to the bus, Yossi said to Josh, "You know, I think I understand something now that I didn't really understand before. In Hebrew, a cemetery is called a *beis hachayim*, which means 'the home for the living.' Now what kind of name is that for a place full of buried people?"

"You're right," Josh agreed. "It is a strange name."

"But it really is the right name because that place was full of life. There were lots of people doing a lot of good things. It felt good to be there. That makes it easier to understand how the neshamos are part of HaShem, and, like Him, they remain alive forever."

33

MY FIRST
MAANEH LASHON

If thirty days have passed since you last visited a cemetery,
say the following blessing when you arrive:

Baruch atah Adonoi Eloheinu melech ha'olam –
Blessed are You, HaShem, our God,
King of the universe,
Who has created you with justice.

בָּרוּךְ אַתָּה יְיָ אֱלֹהֵינוּ
מֶלֶךְ הָעוֹלָם
אֲשֶׁר יָצַר אֶתְכֶם בַּדִּין.

Throughout your life,
He has nourished you
and provided all of your needs with justice,
and He caused your death with justice.
He knows your numbers,
and He will bring you back to life
and keep you alive with justice.

וְזָן אֶתְכֶם בַּדִּין
וְכִלְכֵּל אֶתְכֶם בַּדִּין
וְהֵמִית אֶתְכֶם בַּדִּין.
וְיוֹדֵעַ מִסְפַּר כֻּלְּכֶם
וְהוּא עָתִיד לְהַחֲיוֹתְכֶם
וּלְקַיֵּם אֶתְכֶם בַּדִּין:

Baruch atah Adonoi –
Blessed are You, HaShem,
Who brings the dead back to life.

בָּרוּךְ אַתָּה יְיָ
מְחַיֵּה הַמֵּתִים:

You are mighty forever, HaShem;
You bring the dead back to life;
You are most able to save.
HaShem provides for the living with kindness,
brings back the dead with great mercy,
supports those who fall, heals the sick,
frees those who are bound
and faithfully fulfills His word
to those who have passed away.
Who is like You, Mighty One?
And who can be compared to You, the King,
Who brings about death and brings back to life
and Who brings about salvation?
And You are faithful
to bring the dead back to life.

אַתָּה גִּבּוֹר לְעוֹלָם אֲדֹנָי,
מְחַיֵּה מֵתִים אַתָּה,
רַב לְהוֹשִׁיעַ:
מְכַלְכֵּל חַיִּים בְּחֶסֶד,
מְחַיֵּה מֵתִים בְּרַחֲמִים רַבִּים, סוֹמֵךְ
נוֹפְלִים, וְרוֹפֵא חוֹלִים, וּמַתִּיר
אֲסוּרִים,
וּמְקַיֵּם אֱמוּנָתוֹ
לִישֵׁנֵי עָפָר.
מִי כָמוֹךָ בַּעַל גְּבוּרוֹת
וּמִי דוֹמֶה לָךְ, מֶלֶךְ
מֵמִית וּמְחַיֶּה
וּמַצְמִיחַ יְשׁוּעָה:
וְנֶאֱמָן אַתָּה
לְהַחֲיוֹת מֵתִים:

37

תהילים פרק לג

א רַנְּנוּ צַדִּיקִים בַּיהוָה לַיְשָׁרִים נָאוָה תְהִלָּה:

ב הוֹדוּ לַיהוָה בְּכִנּוֹר בְּנֵבֶל עָשׂוֹר זַמְּרוּ לוֹ:

ג שִׁירוּ לוֹ שִׁיר חָדָשׁ הֵיטִיבוּ נַגֵּן בִּתְרוּעָה:

ד כִּי יָשָׁר דְּבַר יְהוָה וְכָל מַעֲשֵׂהוּ בֶּאֱמוּנָה:

ה אֹהֵב צְדָקָה וּמִשְׁפָּט חֶסֶד יְהוָה מָלְאָה הָאָרֶץ:

ו בִּדְבַר יְהוָה שָׁמַיִם נַעֲשׂוּ וּבְרוּחַ פִּיו כָּל צְבָאָם:

ז כֹּנֵס כַּנֵּד מֵי הַיָּם נֹתֵן בְּאוֹצָרוֹת תְּהוֹמוֹת:

ח יִירְאוּ מֵיהוָה כָּל הָאָרֶץ מִמֶּנּוּ יָגוּרוּ כָּל יֹשְׁבֵי תֵבֵל:

ט כִּי הוּא אָמַר וַיֶּהִי הוּא צִוָּה וַיַּעֲמֹד:

י יְהוָה הֵפִיר עֲצַת גּוֹיִם הֵנִיא מַחְשְׁבוֹת עַמִּים:

יא עֲצַת יְהוָה לְעוֹלָם תַּעֲמֹד מַחְשְׁבוֹת לִבּוֹ לְדֹר וָדֹר:

יב אַשְׁרֵי הַגּוֹי אֲשֶׁר יְהוָה אֱלֹהָיו הָעָם בָּחַר לְנַחֲלָה לוֹ:

יג מִשָּׁמַיִם הִבִּיט יְהוָה רָאָה אֶת כָּל בְּנֵי הָאָדָם:

יד מִמְּכוֹן שִׁבְתּוֹ הִשְׁגִּיחַ אֶל כָּל יֹשְׁבֵי הָאָרֶץ:

טו הַיֹּצֵר יַחַד לִבָּם הַמֵּבִין אֶל כָּל מַעֲשֵׂיהֶם:

טז אֵין הַמֶּלֶךְ נוֹשָׁע בְּרָב חָיִל גִּבּוֹר לֹא יִנָּצֵל בְּרָב כֹּחַ:

יז שֶׁקֶר הַסּוּס לִתְשׁוּעָה וּבְרֹב חֵילוֹ לֹא יְמַלֵּט:

יח הִנֵּה עֵין יְהוָה אֶל יְרֵאָיו לַמְיַחֲלִים לְחַסְדּוֹ:

יט לְהַצִּיל מִמָּוֶת נַפְשָׁם וּלְחַיּוֹתָם בָּרָעָב:

כ נַפְשֵׁנוּ חִכְּתָה לַיהוָה עֶזְרֵנוּ וּמָגִנֵּנוּ הוּא:

כא כִּי בוֹ יִשְׂמַח לִבֵּנוּ כִּי בְשֵׁם קָדְשׁוֹ בָטָחְנוּ:

כב יְהִי חַסְדְּךָ יְהוָה עָלֵינוּ כַּאֲשֶׁר יִחַלְנוּ לָךְ:

Shalom Aleichem, Adoneinu Moreinu V'Rabbeinu

שָׁלוֹם עֲלֵיכֶם אֲדוֹנֵינוּ מוֹרֵינוּ וְרַבֵּינוּ

Peace be unto you, our Masters, our Teachers, and our Rabbis. May you have peace from now and forever.

May you lie in peace in your resting place, and may you not be pained by the troubles of those who are close to you. May you dwell in holiness, and may you rest in the shelter of HaShem.

How fortunate for you and how good it is for you that you merited to follow in the ways of your Creator and to have your light shine forth, that you taught the Jewish people proper laws and good judgments, so that the people of your generation could be righteous. You have much good, and your reward is very great.

May the great and holy King, blessed be He, quickly bring you back to life to rise with all the other tzaddikim and pious men of the world. May He cause you to merit the world that is all good and that has no end and is blessed in every way. May you take pleasure in all the special spiritual rewards, such as the Leviathan at the banquet of Moshiach and the secrets of the Torah, which are compared to good wine, and may you receive the finest of all good in a thousand portions.

Just as you worked hard in this world, occupying yourselves with the words of the Torah, so too may you go from strength to strength, from one heavenly academy to another, reaching a truly awesome place. May you merit to hear from Hashem, blessed be He, new explanations of the Torah that will be revealed in the future.

May it be the will of our Father in Heaven that, in your merit and in the merit of the other tzaddikim and pious men who rest here, I be forgiven for all my sins and the wrongs that I have done.

I have come here out of respect for you, to praise HaShem's great and awesome Name and to daven at your grave. I have come to ask that you pray for me that HaShem protect me from robbery, injury, hardships, fear, worry, a strange and shameful death, and difficult times.

May HaShem bless all that I do with success. May my hurts be healed, my bread and water be blessed, and all sickness be removed from around me. May I be saved from all enemies and people who may want to harm me.

May He provide me, and all the Jewish people, everything that we need to live well in the merit of your righteousness. May He give me a good portion and generous reward so that I merit Olam Haba, and may I merit to hear good news.

May I be granted a long life, years of peace, calm, and security. Let me not be counted among sinners and people who do wrong. May I not die young and may I finish my days in a good old age.

May I be granted increased wisdom, knowledge, and understanding, and may HaShem look upon me with favor, goodness, kindness, and mercy, and may people look upon me with a good eye as well.

May my whole heart be focused on loving HaShem and fearing Him to fulfill His will with a sincere heart.

May He listen to the sound of my davening and not turn me away empty-handed.

The following is a free rhyme paraphrase of the *piyut*
"Ana, Adon HaOlamim" in the *Maaneh Lashon.*
One should lift his eyes heavenward and say:

I ask You, HaShem, Who over all the worlds is King,
As I stand here before You, not hiding anything:

If I made mistakes, committed sins, and did things that are wrong,
Please forgive me and don't be angry with me for long.

Don't leave me alone; that will make things tougher.
I am sorry, and I'll do better; please don't make me suffer.

Please hear my tefillos and listen to me,
Not because I am as good as I can be,

But because in Your kindness You created me with trust
That I will try my best to do what I must.

If I have done wrong, don't judge my bad deed –
Have mercy and help me in my time of need.

You are kind and patient; You want only good,
For the world You created to be safe as it should.

It makes us so happy to know that You care;
You are so understanding and treat us so fair.

If my mistakes have made me seem distant,
I want to come closer, this very instant.

Please help me do teshuvah, so that we'll be reunited.
Draw me closer to You; I'll be so delighted!

Let my tefillos soar up, let nothing interfere;
Accept them, and I will rejoice that we're near.

I may not be deserving, yet please accept my tefillos –
Not in my merit, but in the *zchus* of our *Avos.*

My words may sound simple, not fancy or fine –
Please accept them as tefillos said better than mine,

Like the words of Moshe's song by the sea,
Or David HaMelech's sweet melody.

Let my words be like the songs that the angels sing,
With all the right words, fit for the King.

I have come here because wise people have said
That davening at grave sites is very widespread.

The tzaddik's neshamah can pray for a Jew,
And in doing for others, his neshamah gains, too.

Like a branch that's connected to the trunk of a tree,
Our neshamos are linked like a chain of unity.

Please, HaShem, open Your ears as I pray;
Accept my tefillos, and don't turn me away.

Take my words and my feelings; they're sincere, You can see.
HaShem, You are kind, and You're always there for me.

I ask you, HaShem, that all that I do should be blessed:
I should have enough food and be properly dressed.

I should have all I need and be safe where I go –
You are the One Who can make it so.

If ever I'm lacking the things that I need,
Please give them to me in this way, I plead:

Straight from Your hand so it will be sweet,
Not so that I must take from other people I meet.

Your treasure stores are full; give to me from there,
Because taking from others is shameful to bear.

Grant me a long, healthy life to live;
Bless me that I care for others and always give.

Wherever I am I should make a *kiddush HaShem*.
People should like me and I should like them.

I know You will consider all that I say –
You are kind and listen to those who sincerely pray.

Please, HaShem,
do not turn me away
empty-handed.
May I benefit from the merit of the tzaddikim,
our masters and teachers,
who are buried here
and all over the world, from the merit
of their study of the holy Torah,
the teachings they taught,
and the good deeds they performed
in this world.
May they represent me
before Your throne of glory
so that everything that I,
Your servant, ask for will be fulfilled.
Do not turn me away empty-handed,
and may nothing bad ever get in my way,
now or forever. Amen, selah.

וְאַל תְּשִׁיבֵנִי
רֵיקָם מִלְּפָנֶיךָ
בִּזְכוּת הַצַּדִּיקִים
מָרָנָן וְרַבָּנָן
הַנִּקְבָּרִים פֹּה
וּבְכָל הָעוֹלָם וּבִזְכוּת
תּוֹרָתָם הַקְּדוֹשָׁה
וְחִדּוּשֵׁיהָ שֶׁנִּתְחַדְּשׁוּ עַל יְדֵיהֶם
וּמַעֲשֵׂיהֶם הַטּוֹבִים שֶׁעָשׂוּ
בָּעוֹלָם הַזֶּה.
כֻּלָּם יִהְיוּ עָלַי מְלִיצֵי יֹשֶׁר לְפָנֶיךָ
וְלִפְנֵי כִסֵּא כְבוֹדֶךָ
לַעֲשׂוֹת אֶת שְׁאֵלָתִי וְלִמַלְּאוֹת
אֶת בַּקָּשָׁתִי אֲשֶׁר עַבְדְּךָ מִתְפַּלֵּל לְפָנֶיךָ
לְבִלְתִּי אָשׁוּב רֵיקָם
וְאַל יִמְנָעֵנִי שׁוּם מְקַטְרֵג
מֵעַתָּה וְעַד עוֹלָם אָמֵן סֶלָה:

Now read your "pan" and tear it over the tziyun.

There is much more happening at the Ohel than we can see. We are at a holy grave site, where the tzaddik's neshamah is continuously present and we can connect in a real way. We can learn about how this happens from holy books that explain many secrets of the Torah. The *Zohar*, written by Rabbi Shimon bar Yochai, is one of these books. Here is a passage from the *Zohar* that explains how davening at the grave sites of tzaddikim connects us to them and how the tzaddikim daven for us:

Rabbi Yitzchak says: "The tzaddikim are worthy in this world and in the next, for they are very holy. The body of the tzaddik is holy, his **nefesh** is holy, his **ruach** is holy, his **neshamah** is holy of holies."

We usually think that a person has two parts to him: a body, which we call the "*guf*," and a soul, which we call the "*neshamah*." But Rabbi Yitzchak teaches us that the soul has different parts to it, and the neshamah is just one part. There is also the nefesh and the ruach and other parts, as well as the neshamah.

The nefesh of a tzaddik has not left this world entirely. It is still present and connected to this world, and it knows the pain and hardships of the living. It stays here to protect the living, watching what happens here and then reaching up to higher places to do what it can to help.

When the world is in need of mercy and people are suffering, they go to holy grave sites and ask that the nefesh of the tzaddik daven for them. The nefesh – that part of the tzaddik's soul that has not left this world – can then soar up to higher places. There it connects to the parts of his soul that are more distant from this world. All those parts join in davening and ask for help on behalf of people living in our world.

But this does not happen automatically. We need to prepare ourselves to focus and concentrate on our prayers so that we really mean what we are saying when we go to a holy grave site. The *Zohar* quotes a discussion between great Rabbis about this. They knew that approaching the nefesh of a tzaddik should be taken very seriously, and that not everyone is on the level to be able to do it properly.

The *Zohar* quotes one of those Rabbis, Rabbi Chiya, who would pray for the Jewish people at the resting places of tzaddikim. He was concerned about who would do this after he was no longer alive.

Rabbi Chiya said: "I wonder if anyone knows how to inform the nefesh of a tzaddik who has passed away of people's troubles."

Rabbi Abba replied: "The nefashos (more than one nefesh) of tzaddikim who pass away are sensitive to people's suffering. When there is no one who can inform the nefashos properly, people bring a sefer Torah near their graves. The nefashos are disturbed when a sefer Torah is brought to a *beis hachayim* and ask why it was brought there. An angel called Dumah informs them of the trouble that the Jewish people face."

Rabbi Yosei added: "The nefashos know that the world is in trouble and that the people are not worthy or do not know how to approach them. So the nefashos cry out for the dishonor done to the Torah, which had to be brought to a *beis hachayim*.

"If the people do teshuvah and call out with all their hearts and turn to HaShem, then the nefashos of the tzaddikim gather together and plead for mercy on the people's behalf. The nefashos want to make the tefillos even more powerful. And it is known that all tefillos go up to HaShem through the special gates of prayer at Chevron. So the nefashos of the tzaddikim call upon our *Avos* and *Imahos*, who are buried in Me'aras HaMachpelah in Chevron, and ask them to daven for the people. Our *Avos* and *Imahos* are able to reach very high places in Heaven and can bring about good decrees for the world.

"All this can happen when the living people truly do teshuvah, daven sincerely, and decide to act better. If they don't, then they have done wrong in bringing the sefer Torah to the cemetery and causing the neshamos to gather for nothing. This will not bring good things for the people."

In the *Zohar,* there is a story told by Rabbi Yehudah that helps us understand how real all this is:

One day Rabbi Chizkiyah and Rabbi Yeissa were traveling. They came upon a town called Gush Chalav, which lay in ruins after being attacked in war.

They sat down near the cemetery. Rabbi Yeissa held in his hand a torn portion of a Torah scroll, which he had spotted among the ruins. While they sat there, a grave began to stir nearby, and they heard a cry: "Woe, woe, for the world is in distress! A Torah scroll has been exiled here. Otherwise the living people would not have come here."

Rabbi Chizkiyah and Rabbi Yeissa were startled, and Rabbi Chizkiyah said, "Who are you?"

The voice replied, "I am dead, but I have been awakened by the Torah scroll. It happened that one time the world was in distress, and the living came here to awaken us with a Torah scroll. My companions and I approached the holy graves in Chevron. We were joined by the tzaddikim from Gan Eden. Then it was discovered that the sefer Torah that the living people brought before us had a mistake in it. It did not read exactly as HaShem had dictated and therefore was false. Falsehood cannot be said in the name of the King, and all of us who had caused this holy group to gather for nothing in Gan Eden were sent away. Later, the scribe Rabbi Hamnuna the Elder was instructed to correct the sefer Torah.

"Then Rabbi Elazar, the son of Rabbi Shimon bar Yochai, who was buried with us, was awakened and prayed in Gan Eden and brought blessing into the world. After that, we were given permission to rejoin the gathering.

"Later, the grave of Rabbi Elazar was moved and reburied with his father in Meron. Since then, there is no one among us that has been aroused to approach the holy graves in Chevron. We remember with fear the day my companions and I were sent away. If you are coming to us now with a Torah scroll, the world must be in distress. This worries me, for I wonder: Who will go ahead and tell those truly righteous ones in Chevron?"

Rabbi Chizkiyah replied, "Heaven forbid, the world is not in distress, and we have not come for that purpose."

Then Rabbi Chizkiyah and Rabbi Yeissa rose and went on their way. "It must be," they concluded, "that when there are no righteous people in the world, the world can continue to exist in the *zchus* of those who have passed away."

Rabbi Yeissa said, "This also teaches us why it is proper to go and pray at holy grave sites when there is a drought and the world needs rain. We might have thought this would not be allowed because the Torah commands us not to 'inquire of the dead.' "[35]

Rabbi Chizkiyah said, "But that is speaking about the custom of non-Jewish people to go to graves and try to awaken spirits through magic. Those are graves of people who have sinned and are considered forever dead. But when Jewish people visit holy grave sites, they come while they are fasting and with a heartfelt decision to do teshuvah. They come with sincere *kavanah* to connect with holy neshamos and ask for HaShem's mercy through the *zchus* of their tefillos.

"This is what we have learned: Even when he departs from this world, a tzaddik does not totally rise to the higher world or vanish from any world. He can be found in all the worlds, more than in his lifetime. In his lifetime, he was found only in this world, but afterward he can be found in three worlds and we can connect to him."[36]

The following is a free rhyme paraphrase of the passage *Maavar Yabok* in the *Maaneh Lashon*.

Yehi ratzon milfanecha Adonoi Eloheinu v'Eilohei avoseinu –
May it be Your will, HaShem,
our God and the God of our fathers:

We ask for Your kindness and mercy and care.
Brighten our lives; save us from despair.

Keep us away from things that are bad,
From what people have said or cruel thoughts that they had.

Let there be no hate or jealousy of others.
Let us love each other like sisters and brothers.

Let our homes be places of learning and growing,
Full of Torah and *yiras Shamayim* and goodness, ongoing.

Help me have a good heart, a good eye, and a good name,
Good friends and a strong *yetzer tov* that won't cause me shame.

I should make a *kiddush HaShem* wherever I go.
I should act the right way, and it will clearly show.

You know that I really want to do good,
And You also want me to do as I should.

It's just the *yetzer hara* that gets in the way –
You know how hard it can be to obey.

He is so tricky he makes my head spin.
Please give me strength so I won't give in.

If I make mistakes, I ask: Please forgive,
And bless us that in *ahavas Yisrael* we should live

תהילים פרק צא

א יֹשֵׁב בְּסֵתֶר עֶלְיוֹן בְּצֵל שַׁדַּי יִתְלוֹנָן:

ב אֹמַר לַיהוָה מַחְסִי וּמְצוּדָתִי אֱלֹהַי אֶבְטַח בּוֹ:

ג כִּי הוּא יַצִּילְךָ מִפַּח יָקוּשׁ מִדֶּבֶר הַוּוֹת:

ד בְּאֶבְרָתוֹ יָסֶךְ לָךְ וְתַחַת כְּנָפָיו תֶּחְסֶה צִנָּה
וְסֹחֵרָה אֲמִתּוֹ:

ה לֹא תִירָא מִפַּחַד לָיְלָה מֵחֵץ יָעוּף יוֹמָם:

ו מִדֶּבֶר בָּאֹפֶל יַהֲלֹךְ מִקֶּטֶב יָשׁוּד צָהֳרָיִם:

ז יִפֹּל מִצִּדְּךָ אֶלֶף וּרְבָבָה מִימִינֶךָ אֵלֶיךָ לֹא יִגָּשׁ:

ח רַק בְּעֵינֶיךָ תַבִּיט וְשִׁלֻּמַת רְשָׁעִים תִּרְאֶה:

ט כִּי אַתָּה יְהוָה מַחְסִי עֶלְיוֹן שַׂמְתָּ מְעוֹנֶךָ:

י לֹא תְאֻנֶּה אֵלֶיךָ רָעָה וְנֶגַע לֹא יִקְרַב בְּאָהֳלֶךָ:

יא כִּי מַלְאָכָיו יְצַוֶּה לָּךְ לִשְׁמָרְךָ בְּכָל דְּרָכֶיךָ:

יב עַל כַּפַּיִם יִשָּׂאוּנְךָ פֶּן תִּגֹּף בָּאֶבֶן רַגְלֶךָ:

יג עַל שַׁחַל וָפֶתֶן תִּדְרֹךְ תִּרְמֹס כְּפִיר וְתַנִּין:

יד כִּי בִי חָשַׁק וַאֲפַלְּטֵהוּ אֲשַׂגְּבֵהוּ כִּי יָדַע שְׁמִי:

טו יִקְרָאֵנִי וְאֶעֱנֵהוּ עִמּוֹ אָנֹכִי בְצָרָה אֲחַלְּצֵהוּ
וַאֲכַבְּדֵהוּ:

טז אֹרֶךְ יָמִים אַשְׂבִּיעֵהוּ וְאַרְאֵהוּ בִּישׁוּעָתִי:

Yehi ratzon milfanecha Adonoi Eloheinu v'Eilohei avoseinu –

May it be Your will, HaShem,	יְהִי רָצוֹן מִלְפָנֶיךָ יְיָ
our God and the God of our fathers,	אֱלֹהֵינוּ וֵאלֹהֵי אֲבוֹתֵינוּ
that You grant us long life,	שֶׁתִּתֵּן לָנוּ חַיִּים אֲרוּכִים.
a life of peace, a life of goodness,	חַיִּים שֶׁל שָׁלוֹם. חַיִּים שֶׁל טוֹבָה.
a life of blessing, a life without lack,	חַיִּים שֶׁל בְּרָכָה. חַיִּים שֶׁל פַּרְנָסָה.
a life of health,	חַיִּים שֶׁל חִלּוּץ עֲצָמוֹת.
a life of fear of sin,	חַיִּים שֶׁיֵּשׁ בָּהֶם יִרְאַת חֵטְא.
a life without shame and disgrace,	חַיִּים שֶׁאֵין בָּהֶם בּוּשָׁה
a life full of plenty of the things that we need,	וּכְלִמָּה.
a life of wealth and honor,	חַיִּים שֶׁל עֹשֶׁר וְכָבוֹד.
a life in which the love of Torah	חַיִּים שֶׁתְּהֵא בָנוּ אַהֲבַת תּוֹרָה
and yiras Shamayim fills our hearts,	וְיִרְאַת שָׁמַיִם.
a life in which You will fulfill	חַיִּים שֶׁתְּמַלֵּא לָנוּ
all the desires of our hearts in a good way.	כָּל מִשְׁאֲלוֹת לִבֵּנוּ לְטוֹבָה

Please answer our prayers	
in the merits of the Tannaim and	בִּזְכוּת הַתַּנָּאִים
the Amoraim,	וְהָאֲמוֹרָאִים
holy men	זְרוֹעוֹת וִירָכִין בְּסִטְרָא דְּקֻדְשָׁה
who are in a strong position above	אֲשֶׁר אִיתָן מוֹשָׁבָם
and in the merit of the tzaddikim	וּבִזְכוּת הַצַּדִּיקִים
who are buried in this place;	הַקְּבוּרִים בַּמָּקוֹם הַזֶּה.
and particularly in the merit of the tzaddikim –	וּבִפְרָט זְכוּת הַצַּדִּיקִים
Adoneinu Moreinu V'Rabbeinu	אֲדוֹנֵינוּ מוֹרֵינוּ וְרַבֵּינוּ
Rabbi **Yosef Yitzchak**;	רַבִּי יוֹסֵף יִצְחָק
the son of Adoneinu Moreinu V'Rabbeinu	בֶּן אֲדוֹנֵינוּ מוֹרֵנוּ וְרַבֵּינוּ
Rabbi **Shalom Dov Ber**;	רַבִּי שָׁלוֹם דֹּב בֶּער
and Adoneinu Moreinu V'Rabbeinu	וַאֲדוֹנֵינוּ מוֹרֵנוּ וְרַבֵּנוּ
Rabbi **Menachem Mendel**,	רַבִּי מְנַחֵם מֶענְדְל
the son of Rabbi **Levi Yitzchak**.	בֶּן הָרַב רַבִּי לֵוִי יִצְחָק
May their zchus protect us	זְכוּתָם יָגֵן עָלֵינוּ
and all the members of our families...	וְעַל כָּל בְּנֵי בֵּיתֵנוּ...

Some people walk out of the Ohel backward out of respect.
Now you can put on your regular shoes.
Wash your hands as you do when washing netilas yadayim in the morning.
When you leave the beis hachayim, you should say:

Yehi ratzon milfanecha Adonoi Elohei v'Eilohei avosei –

May it be Your will, HaShem,	יְהִי רָצוֹן מִלְפָנֶיךָ יְיָ
our God and the God of our fathers,	אֱלֹהַי וֵאלֹהֵי אֲבוֹתַי
that all that I have asked of You	כָּל מַה שֶׁבִּקַשְׁתִּי לְפָנֶיךָ
be viewed as pleasantly as a *ketores* offering.	יִהְיֶה בְּעֵינֶיךָ כִּקְטֹרֶת
Please be lenient with me	וְתַעֲשֶׂה עִמִּי לְפְנִים
and judge me beyond the letter of the law.	מִשׁוּרַת הַדִּין
You are full of kindness,	וְאַתָּה רַחֲמָן
and You listen willingly	שׁוֹמֵעַ בְּרָצוֹן
to the tefillos of Your servant.	תְּפִלַת עַבְדֶךָ
I have come before You	וּבַעֲבוּר זֶה בָּאתִי לְפָנֶיךָ
on my own, without people	כִּי אֵין לִי מֵלִיץ
who will speak up for me.	לְהָלִיץ בַּעֲדִי לְפָנֶיךָ
Do not turn me away	וְנָא אַל תְּשִׁיבֵנִי
from Your presence empty-handed,	רֵיקָם מִלְפָנֶיךָ
for You listen to prayers –	כִּי אַתָּה שׁוֹמֵעַ תְּפִלָה
for the sake of all the tzaddikim	בַּעֲבוּר כָּל הַצַּדִיקִים
resting here	וְהַשׁוֹכְנִים בְּכָאן
and for the sake of Your great honor.	וּבַעֲבוּר תִּפְאַרְתְּךָ הַגָּדוֹל
Blessed is He who hears tefillah.	בָּרוּךְ שׁוֹמֵעַ תְּפִלָה.

Yiheyu l'ratzon imrei fi v'hegyon libi lefanecha Adonoi tzuri v'go'ali –

May the words of my mouth	יִהְיוּ לְרָצוֹן אִמְרֵי פִי,
and the thoughts of my heart	וְהֶגְיוֹן לִבִּי
be acceptable before You,	לְפָנֶיךָ,
HaShem, my Rock and my Redeemer.	יְיָ צוּרִי וְגֹאֲלִי:

**This book is published
in everlasting memory of**

HaRav HaTomim Reb Menachem Mendel
ben HaRav HaTomim Reb Benzion Shemtov

נפטר י״ג ניסן תשס״ו

and his wife Sarah bas Reb Yaakov Efraim HaCohen

נפטרה ז׳ אלול תש״ע

who served as exemplars of hiskashrus to the Rebbe

*Dedicated by their children, grandchildren,
and great-grandchildren*

Glossary

ahavas Yisrael – love for all Jews.

Avos – the forefathers, Avraham, Yitzchak, and Yaakov.

Beis HaMikdash – Holy Temple that stood in Jerusalem over 2,000 years ago.

berachah – blessing.

davening – praying.

dvar Torah – literally, "word of Torah"; a Torah discourse.

Eretz Yisrael – the Land of Israel.

farbrengen – a chassidic gathering where Torah is discussed.

Frierdike Rebbe – the sixth Lubavitcher Rebbe, Rabbi Yosef Yitzchak Schneerson.

gartel – belt worn by chassidim during prayer and other formal occasions.

HaKadosh Baruch Hu – the Holy One, blessed is He.

halachah – Jewish law.

hiskashrus – connection.

kapote – long frock coat.

kavanah – focus and concentration.

ketores – incense offering.

kiddush HaShem – sanctifying G-d's Name.

kohen (plural: *kohanim*) – priest, who is chosen to serve in the Holy Temple; a descendent of Aharon.

Kosel – the Western Wall in Jerusalem, a part of the ancient wall that surrounded the Temple Mount which remains from the destruction and is a holy site for prayer.

geulah – redemption.

Me'aras HaMachpelah – the Cave of Machpelah, where Adam and Chavah, Avraham and Sarah, Yitzchak and Rivkah, and Yaakov and Leah are buried.

mikvah – ritual pool used for immersion and purification.

neshamah (plural: *neshamos*) – the soul.

netilas yadayim – hand washing for ritual purposes.

sefer Torah – Torah scroll.

Talmud – the oral tradition of Jewish law, written down and compiled as the Mishnah and Gemara.

Tatie – father.

tefillah (plural: *tefillos*) – prayer.

Tehillim – Psalms written by King David and often recited as prayers.

teshuvah – repentance.

tzaddik (plural: *tzaddikim*) – a righteous person.

tzedakah – money for charity.

yetzer hara – evil inclination.

yetzer tov – good inclination.

yiras Shamayim – fear of G-d.

Zaidy – grandfather.

zchus – merit.

Zohar – the major kabbalistic work by Rabbi Shimon bar Yochai.

References

1. *Rashi, Bamidbar* 13:22.
2. *Sichos Yud Shvat* 5714.
3. The Rebbe's *Igros Kodesh*, vol. 5, p. 95.
4. Rebbe Rashab, cited in *Sefer HaSichos* 5703, p. 165.
5. See *Ralbag* on *Melachim* II 23:17.
6. *Iyov* 29:3.
7. Rebbe Yisaschar Dov of Dinov, *Agrah LaKallah, parshas Korach.*
8. See Rambam, *Hilchos Yesodei HaTorah* 7:6.
9. *Zohar* II:204b.
10. *Ma'amar Atah Tetzaveh, Sefer Ma'amarim Melukat* 6.
11. *Zohar* III:71a, quoted in *Tanya, Iggeres HaKodesh*, ch. 27.
12. The Rebbe's *Igros Kodesh*, vol. 3, p. 458.
13. Ibid.
14. *Sichos Yud Shvat* 5714.
15. Ibid.
16. The Rebbe's *Igros Kodesh*, vol. 4, no. 1, 138.
17. Tanya, *Iggeres HaKodesh*, Letter no. 27.
18. *Kuntres Hishtatchus; Mishnah Brurah* 559:41; *Be'er Heitev* 581:17.
19. See *Kuntres Hishtatchus.*
20. Ibid.
21. *Sichos Yud Shvat* 5714.
22. Ibid.
23. See *Kesubos* 111a; *Sichah Yud Shvat* 5714 (1954); *Sichah Vav Teves* 5746.
24. The Rebbe's *Igros Kodesh*, vol. 19, p. 396.
25. *Sichos Yud Shvat* 5716; *Likutei Sichos*, vol. 2, p. 503.
26. *Bava Kama* 16b.
27. A comment of the Rebbe to *Igros Kodesh* of the Rebbe Rayatz, vol. 6, p. 292.
28. See *Sefer HaMinhagim*, p. 96.
29. *Likutei Sichos*, vol. 25, p. 502.
30. The Rebbe's *Igros Kodesh,* vol. 11, p. 154.
31. The Rebbe's *Igros Kodesh,* vol. 19, p. 414.
32. *Mishlei* 20:27.
33. See *Ramban, Shmos* 28:35. See also *Toras Menachem, Reshimas HaYoman*, p. 266; *Likkutei Dibburim* (Eng. Ed.), vol. 4, p. 21.
34. *Mishlei* 16:1.
35. *Devarim* 18:10.
36. *Zohar* III:70b ff.